QE2
FINAL WESTBOUND CROSSING

CHRISTOPHER WALLACE

Foreword by Ian McNaught CVO MNM FNI

Photographs by Ian Wilson

Additional Photographs by QE2's
Onboard Photographic Team

Cover Photograph by: Ian Wilson
Book design by: SWATT Books Ltd

Printed in the United Kingdom
First Printing, 2022

ISBN: 978-1-7392136-0-2 (Paperback)
ISBN: 978-1-7392136-1-9 (eBook)

Christopher Wallace
United Kingdom
clydebuilt736@gmail.com

This book is dedicated
to my Mum Patricia

Sunday 24th September 1967

QE2 in Fitting-Out Basin of John Brown & Co. Ltd

Shipbuilder: Clydebank Scotland

Foreword

There is something very special about a transatlantic crossing. It is not a cruise, there are no ports of call on the way, just you and the North Atlantic and four days at sea, and to enjoy the very last westbound crossing from Southampton to New York on *QE2* was very special for all of us, crew, and passengers alike.

In the golden days of Cunard, in the 1950s, the *Queens Mary* and *Elizabeth* used to meet each other mid-Atlantic on their weekly schedule but never sailed in tandem. This final crossing in October 2008 was in tandem with our big sister *Queen Mary 2*, fine company for a Clyde-built thoroughbred who could still show her heels to the young pretender, even as she was preparing to retire after thirty-nine years of service.

Some could have looked at that crossing with sadness but it was to be a celebration. A celebration of the last British-built Atlantic liner, a celebration of the ship's company whose home she had become over all those years and a celebration of her passengers who had sailed all around the world in her and enjoyed the unique experience she offered.

Some of those passengers were there for the first time, just in time to enjoy this classic liner and all that she exemplified. We shall never see the likes of her again, so join Christopher and Ian on that crossing and enjoy the greatest ship in the world in her true element of the North Atlantic.

Captain Ian McNaught CVO MNM FNI
Final Master, QE2

Contents

Introduction

My favourite photograph of the *QE2* was taken on Sunday 24th of September 1967, at John Brown's shipyard in Clydebank Scotland – four days after her launch by HM Queen Elizabeth II. This photograph shows the *QE2* docked in the Fitting-Out Basin at John Brown's shipyard. Her red keel and rudder are visible above the waterline, implying not much – if anything – had yet been installed in her.

This photograph shows me standing at the edge of a wheat field at Old Mains Farm, outside the village of Inchinnan in Renfrewshire, on the opposite bank of the River Clyde facing the basin, with my three brothers and my maternal Uncle James standing with me. I am the six-year-old small dark-haired boy in the green anorak (without a woollen hat), with my right arm raised in salute to the new Cunarder.

I remember thinking when I saw her, that I was pleased she now had a name – no longer would she be referred to only by her build number of "736".

I have had an interest in Cunard's liners ever since I learnt as a very young boy that my paternal grandfather had worked as a riveter at John Brown's shipyard in Clydebank during the building of RMS *Queen Mary* in the early 1930's.

My Uncle James had often told me how – as a fourteen-year-old boy – he and some school friends cycled from his home in Bridgton Glasgow, to the top of Dumbarton Rock, which is a plug of volcanic basalt 240 feet high and located to the west of Clydebank, further down the river from Brown's shipyard. From this height, it gave Uncle James and his school friends a birds-eye view to watch the new RMS *Queen Mary* sail past, bound for Greenock and her subsequent sea trials, prior to sailing to Southampton from where she would depart on her maiden voyage to New York in May 1936.

I remember saying to my Mum when I got home that afternoon after seeing the new liner. "When I grow up, I want to sail on the *QE2* to New York."

As it turned out – I had a long wait.

It was forty-one years later that my wish came true, on what turned out to be the *QE2's* final westbound crossing to New York in October 2008. I had received a letter from Cunard in the summer of 2007, answering my enquiry – for some "general information" on Cunard's ships and their voyages for the coming year.

I was shocked to read in this letter that the *QE2* had been sold to a consortium in Dubai.

"You cannot sell her, I have not sailed on her yet!" I panicked, on reading this disturbing news.

I immediately sent an email to Cunard attempting to book passage on her. I got a reply a few days later from Cunard saying: "Unfortunately, the *QE2* is fully booked, but if we get a cancellation we will be in touch." I crossed my fingers, said a lot of prayers, and waited anxiously.

My prayers were answered about a week or so later, when another email from Cunard landed in my Inbox, stating that they had received a cancellation and they were now able to offer me and my friend Ian a stateroom on the *QE2*'s final westbound crossing to New York.

It was a life-long dream come true for me; I was a very happy man. I accepted their offer and began counting down the months until our departure the following year.

As I made plans for the sailing; I compiled a list of what I wanted to see whilst we were on board the *QE2*.

Top of this list; was seeing the "builder's plate"; which is a plaque made by John Brown's, stating that the *QE2* was: "built and engined by John Brown & Company Ltd. of Clydebank Scotland."

I had seen pictures in books of similar builder's plates on her sister Cunard ships RMS *Queen Mary* and RMS *Queen Elizabeth*. Therefore, I assumed the *QE2* had one also – I just had to find it.

CHAPTER 1:

Sailing Day

Friday, 10th October 2008

Weather: Sunny

Our day of departure finally arrived and Ian and I travelled down to Southampton and entered the Queen Elizabeth II Terminal, which had been decorated with many Union Jack flags hanging from inside the entrance-hall roof of the terminal. We joined a large queue inside the terminal to confirm our booking at one of the many ticket desks; which were each adorned with a Cunard sign above each desk.

After booking in, we were instructed to go to a large seating area and wait to be called to board the *QE2*. As we waited on our call, I could not believe that I was *finally* and after all these years, about to board the *QE2* and sail on her to New York.

My memory of seeing her in John Brown's Fitting-Out basin in Clydebank a few days after her launch came flooding back to me and now all this seemed so unreal. I looked again at our ticket in the handsome Cunard wallet in my hand and I shook my head in disbelief.

"Please don't let this be a dream," I said to Ian.

Entrance Hall of the Queen Elizabeth II Terminal

He confirmed to me that it was not a dream.

Sailing in tandem with us across the North Atlantic Ocean on this voyage was Cunard's flagship RMS *Queen Mary 2*.

Passengers were allowed to board from 1PM. Our stateroom was on Four Deck, which was the third and lowest deck of passenger accommodation staterooms on the *QE2* on this voyage, so naturally, we had to wait sometime until our boarding pass number was called over tannoy system.

Eventually, our boarding number was called and we both stood up, took a deep breath, and followed our fellow passengers to the departure gate. We made our way up a ramp to the gangway which led out to the *QE2*.

Outside the windows on the right-hand side of this ramp, was the *QE2* herself, lying docked at the side of the QEII Terminal – her bow facing south. As I approached the open shell door in the side of the *QE2* at the end of

QE2 docked outside the QE II Terminal

the gangway, I paused to pat the metal plate of her hull at the side of the doorway. I had wanted to touch her ever since I was a small boy.

"Hello *QE2*," I said to her. "You're taking Ian and me to New York!"

We entered the Midship Lobby through this doorway and were greeted by the beautiful sounds of a large gold-coloured harp being played by the harpist: Sian Williams. I had never heard a harp being played live before and it added an air of enchantment to the occasion. The walls of the Midship Lobby were decorated with magnificent large black and white prints of some of Cunard's famous liners from the past: The *Queens Mary* and *Elizabeth*, RMS *Mauretania*, and RMS *Aquitania*.

There were also many famous buildings in the background of each print which included; The Empire State Building in New York, an airship flying over the Chrysler Building on the island of Manhattan's eastern side and even the *QE2* herself was here, depicted alongside the Sydney Opera House down under in

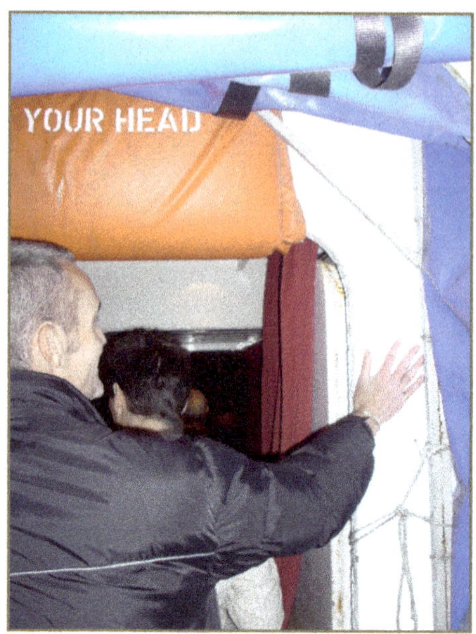

"Hello QE2"

Australia. Another painting showed Concorde flying over the *QE2* departing New York by The Twin Towers on the southern tip of Manhattan Island.

Cunard's most famous liners were on every wall – I was in my element! We were introduced to our cabin steward, who took us to a nearby lift and down to our stateroom – which had its own porthole! Our stateroom was on the port (left hand) side of the ship – looking towards her bow.

In the bygone days of ocean liner travel, a stateroom this low down would have been known as travelling in "steerage." But our stateroom was a far cry from the "steerage" days of yesteryear. As you entered the stateroom, on the right-hand side was a passageway which led to two large wardrobes and a toilet with a shower.

It was a comfortably-sized room with two single beds. A dressing table with a tall mirror above it was set between the beds. Another full-length mirror hung on the wall opposite the beds. A small television set sat on a movable shelf on the wall opposite the beds. This shelf could be swung left or right to ensure a clear view of the tv for both of us from the comfort of our beds, if we wanted to watch a film or whatever was on one of the 18 channels. A television programme guide was placed on the dressing table for our use. The only channel I ever watched with interest over the next five and a half days was Channel 6 – which showed the time and *QE2's* position on the North Atlantic Ocean.

A bonus in sailing westward was that the clocks were put back an hour every night, which meant that if we wanted to, we could stay up an hour later each night of the voyage.

We went back up to the open helideck towards the rear of the ship and mingled with the crowd of passengers who were all enjoying complimentary glasses of champagne. We joined them in singing along to *Rule Britannia*, which was being played over the ship's tannoy system. A wave of patriotism washed over me as the reality of what was happening sank in.

Here I stood on the deck of the last British-built Cunard Ocean liner which had been built by the world-renowned shipyard of John Brown & Company Ltd in Clydebank Scotland and we were about to sail across the North Atlantic Ocean to New York in the United States of America.

The shipyard of John Brown & Company in Clydebank was historically the Cunard Line's preferred choice of shipbuilder. It built amongst others: RMS *Lusitania*; RMS *Aquitania*; RMS *Queen Mary* & RMS *Queen Elizabeth*, as well as HMY *Britannia* and many famous Royal Navy vessels. I felt truly humbled to be a passenger on the *Queen Elizabeth 2* – yet another great Clyde-built liner.

"We're moving!" I exclaimed; seeing a gap appear in the water between the ship and the dock.

Our voyage had begun.

I gripped the handrail in excitement and turned to my left to see *Queen Mary 2* sailing slowly behind us down Southampton Water. *QE2's* whistle sounded

Queen Mary 2 follows QE2 down Southampton Water

in deference to the QM2 – who was Cunard's flagship. It was as if she was communicating with the *QM2*, that she too, was now on her way. We cleared the Queen Elizabeth II Cruise Terminal to the strains of *Land of Hope and Glory* coming over the ship's tannoy – our St. Andrew's Cross flag was draped proudly over the railing which edged the deck and was gently fluttering in the breeze. Our flag was a tribute to the world-famous shipyard in Clydebank which had built this great ship.

We set sail for New York at just after 5PM.

The two liners sailed slowly down Southampton Water, before entering the Solent – which is a busy straight of water between the Isle of Wight and the English mainland. Both ships sailed past Nab Tower which is a tower planned for anti-submarine protection in the Solent during World War I. It was sunk over the Nab rocks, east of the Isle of Wight and is a well-known landmark for sailors as it marks the deep-water eastern entry into the Solent. We sailed by Nab Tower and parallel to the eastern coast of the Isle of Wight, before turning and sailing west through the English Channel towards Bishop's Rock where the North Atlantic is judged to begin.

As we were on an *"early sitting,"* we returned to our stateroom. Our dinner was at 6.15PM in the Mauretania Restaurant, which was on the upper deck – four decks below and directly underneath the *QE2*'s mast.

The first night's dress code for dinner was semi-formal dress: this required a jacket, shirt, and tie with casual trousers for men and either a cocktail dress or trouser suit for ladies. Cunard's dress code required that items of denim clothing should not be worn for dining. This was the first time for both Ian and myself that we had ever gone on holiday and not taken a pair of denims to wear. We each had a shower and unpacked a jacket, chinos and a shirt and tie to wear for dinner. Once suitably dressed, we made our way up to the Mauretania Restaurant.

As we entered the restaurant, we could not help but notice the extravagant centrepiece of this room: an impressive statue of three wild horses heads in the surf by the sculptress, Anthea Wynne. We made our way to our designated table, where two of the waiting staff pushed our chairs under us as we sat down. Then two of them each took an ornately folded napkin off the table and with a deft flick, opened the napkin and spread it across our laps before handing each of us a commemorative menu for that evening's dinner.

This night's menu card had on the cover; a photograph of the *QE2* leaving Southampton on her Maiden Voyage, her *first* westbound crossing to New York on 2nd May 1969. Looking at this photograph highlighted to me the sad fact that this menu was for dinner on the first night of her *last* westbound crossing to New York.

Choosing what to eat was not easy as it all seemed mouth-watering and that was just reading the menu! I settled for smoked trout mousse quenelle on pumpernickel toast and salad bouquet for my starter. The main course was a grilled sirloin steak of Angus beef with a truffle burgundy glaze with string beans, broiled Provençal tomato and Lyonnaise potatoes. Desert was profiteroles with passion fruit mousse and coconut ice cream.

To sum up the meal, I can only think of one description: It was *most delicious*! Each mouthful seemed to be tastier than the previous one.

I had heard about just how good the food on the *QE2* was, but I was very impressed at just how good it was. The serving staff treated us both as if we were Royalty and they were very polite, friendly and incredibly courteous. They were all extremely efficient and so very capable at their jobs. Our wine waiter was a friendly young Frenchman called Jean, whose wine recommendation was the perfect complement to our meal.

After dinner, we went back to our stateroom and unpacked and we then set off to explore the *QE2*. I must have asked every member of the crew whom I met that evening, if they knew where the builder's plate was. The answer to my query was almost the same from everyone I asked: "I don't know" or "I've never heard of the builder's plate." Undeterred, I thought: "Well, I've got another five days on board – surely, I'll meet someone who will know where it is."

We did find The Golden Lion Pub on the same deck as the Mauretania Restaurant. It was situated amidships: four decks directly below the funnel. Ray Terry and his Jazz Band were The Golden Lion's resident band every evening of the crossing and entertained everyone with a collection of musical jazz classics. After a pint of beer to quench our thirsts, we headed to the Yacht Club Bar which was also on the upper deck – overlooking the stern. From 8.45 p.m. till late, DJ Gary King was the entertainment here, with a Caribbean band called "*Changez*" providing the DJ with a break during his set.

We eventually called it a night at 2.30AM and headed back to our stateroom and our beds. The walk down the alleyway to our stateroom – which was not far from the bow – was a rather unsteady affair; which had more to do with the rough sea which the *QE2* was now sailing through, rather than the alcohol which we had consumed that evening. The ship's builders had thoughtfully attached handrails to the left-hand wall of the alleyway, which we both appreciated.

We reached our stateroom and thankfully got into our beds. The *QE2* was pitching and rocking through the sea so much, that just before I closed my eyes, I thought: "I hope she stays in one piece!" Then, I reminded myself – that as she was "*Clyde-built*" – she was more than capable of handling this rough sea. I patted the wall at the side of my bed and said "Good night and safe sailing QE2." With that comforting thought, I closed my eyes and fell asleep.

CHAPTER 2

Our first full day at sea

Saturday, 11th October 2008

Weather: sunny and very calm sea.

Breakfast in the Mauretania Restaurant lived up to the reputation set by the previous night's evening meal. After a bowl of cereal and an enjoyable full English breakfast, plus mushrooms, toast and several cups of very tasty coffee, the first order of the day was a visit to the launderette. We went there to iron our dress shirts for that week's evening meals – a requirement for formal dress. This evening's meal required a suit and bow tie, complete with cufflinks for our neatly ironed shirts and an ironed handkerchief for our breast pockets to complete the outfits.

We returned to our stateroom, carefully hanging our freshly-ironed shirts in the wardrobes. I put on the television and selected Channel 6 to see where we were on the Atlantic. The British mainland and the Isles of Scilly were now behind us and we were sailing on the North Atlantic Ocean. The screen informed me that the time was 10.30AM and the *QE2* was cruising at 22.4 knots and was situated almost in a direct line south of the Old Head of Kinsale headland on the south coast of Ireland.

I reflected for a moment on the sobering thought that it was off the Old Head of Kinsale that the QE2's acclaimed Cunard ancestor RMS *Lusitania* was torpedoed by a German U-boat in 1915 and sank with a great loss of life. I was brought back to the present day, by Ian asking me where my video camera was – as we were going to walk around the ship's Boat Decks. The *QE2* was the only ocean liner in existence that it was possible to walk outside entirely around the ship from bow to stern. I picked up my video camera and eagerly followed Ian to the lift and we travelled up to the portside Boat Deck.

When we came out of the lift onto the Boat Deck, we were impressed to see the figurehead of *Britannia*, which used to grace the bow on Cunard's first transatlantic ship: the paddle steamer RMS *Britannia*. She had made her maiden voyage on 4th July 1840, leaving from Liverpool and arriving in Halifax, Nova Scotia in Canada on July 17th; thus starting Cunard's long and profitable service of transatlantic travel between Great Britain and the continent of North America.

In a glass display case opposite the figurehead of *Britannia*, was a large model of Cunard's SS *Russia*. The "SS *Russia*" had been built by J & G Thomson Shipbuilders of Clydebank in 1867. She was the last Cunarder to be built with a clipper bow and a figurehead. She was a fine-looking "single-stacker" (one funnel) and had a fast speed – for the time – of 14 knots. During the Anglo-Zulu War of 1879, she served as a troopship. The writer Charles Dickens returned to England on the *Russia* after his second tour of the United States and he was full of praise for the ship.

We found a door which led us outside onto the portside Boat Deck. It was very windy outside – after the relative calm of the *QE2*'s interior. Above us to our left, hung No.2 lifeboat which was painted in red to signify that it was for the use of crew members only.

We turned right and headed to a flight of stairs which led up to the Sun Deck which overlooked the *QE2*'s bow. It was much windier up here. Standing overlooking the bow of the *QE2* was quite a special moment for me; although I was unaware at this time, that I would experience many more special moments on this voyage.

Figurehead from RMS Britannia

Forward portside Boat Deck

Steps leading up to forward Sun Deck

The author on the forward Sun Deck overlooking QE2's bow

Calm Atlantic as viewed from above on forward Sun Deck

Impressive background

Forward starboard Boat Deck

In the centre of the metal panel which edged the Sun Deck and overlooked a crane on the bow, was the Cunard logo – a golden lion with a crown on its head, holding a globe of the world. This image signified Cunard's royal status as a carrier of mail across the world's oceans.

The sea was very calm. *Queen Mary 2* sailed off the *QE2*'s starboard bow and a large blue-hulled container ship ploughed through the ocean some distance behind *QM2* and to the north of her starboard stern. The cloudy skies above us ended almost in a straight line from north to south above *QE2* and *QM2*. Ahead of both ships, the sky was totally clear of clouds with nothing but clear blue skies for as far as the eye could see.

As we cleared the cloudy sky, the sun bathed down on both Cunard ships with brilliant sunshine. We made our way down the steep steps from the Sun Deck to the starboard Boat Deck. We marvelled at the very calm sea all around us. This was not the Atlantic Ocean I had been expecting and had seen in countless photographs, on films and television.

RMS Queen Mary 2

I have an old book at home called *Ships of the Cunard Line* by Frank E Dodman, which has a photograph of RMS *Queen Mary* sailing westbound through a very angry Atlantic in 1942. In the photograph, the sea was coming right over her bow and drenching her bridge superstructure. *This* was the Atlantic Ocean I had been expecting to see on this voyage; certainly not such a calm sea with the only white waves to be seen, being caused by the *QE2* and the *QM2* as they both cut through the ocean in a stately and steady manner.

Most Americans refer to the ocean between our two countries as "*The Pond.*" That nickname was very appropriate today– and – as it turned out – almost throughout the entire voyage. It stayed very calm and pond-like for most of the way across the North Atlantic to New York.

By the time we had completely walked around the Boat Decks – ending our stroll back at the Sun Deck underneath the bridge – the sun had disappeared once more under cloudy skies and we made our way down the steps again to the starboard Boat Deck. We then walked all the way to her stern, where we were delighted to see a pod of whale's swim by the portside of the ship.

They were blowing air up through their blowholes. When the warm air from inside their bodies meets the much cooler temperature of the air outside, it immediately condenses, making it look like a spout of water. "At least we're not alone," I said to Ian, nodding towards the whales.

Apart from *QM2* and the cargo ship which we had seen earlier that afternoon, you could be forgiven for thinking that we were indeed alone, with nothing but sea all around us in every direction. Obviously, we had Captain McNaught, his crew and our fellow passengers for company. But all things considered, it still was strange being so isolated out on the North Atlantic Ocean.

The two of us had never been this far out to sea before. Both of us were used to living and working in busy environments with lots of people around us. This daily solitude was something totally new and to be honest, it did take a bit of getting used to.

As we made our way around the ship again, we ended up at H stairway, which was to be found a short walk from the stern between One & Five Decks. The walls of this staircase were lined with paintings of some of Cunard's most famous liners, starting with the *QE2* herself, plus the *Caronia*, looking splendid in her green livery, then the *Queens Mary & Elizabeth*.

A painting of *"Lizzie"* showed the *Queen Mary II* – a well-known pleasure steamer in Scotland, who used to ferry tourists around the Western Isles and Highland ports of Scotland. This painting showed the pleasure steamer sitting alongside *RMS Queen Elizabeth*. This was on the occasion when Her Majesty Queen Elizabeth, (latterly known as the Queen Mother), and her daughters, Princess Elizabeth, and Princess Margaret were visiting RMS *Queen Elizabeth* following her refit after World War Two. *"Lizzie"* was about to embark on her sea trials off the Isle of Arran – which lies off the west coast of Scotland.

RMS Aquitania leaving Pier 54 on the Hudson River

On the opposite wall was a painting by Harley Crossley of RMS *Lusitania* leaving Liverpool on her maiden voyage in 1907. Continuing down the stairs, we came across a painting of RMS *Aquitania* leaving the Cunard Pier 54 – on the island of Manhattan in New York.

H Staircase – one of the smallest staircases on the *QE2* – also had a painting of the *Queens' Mary* and *Elizabeth* passing each other mid-Atlantic.

Another painting showed the *QE2* leaving Manhattan with Concorde flying high above her – just like the large black and white print which adorned one of the walls of the Midship Lobby – with the Statue of Liberty in the foreground, beside another painting of the *Caronia* docked in Cape Town in South Africa with Table Mountain rising majestically in the background. These paintings were quite a historical collection to view and showed many of Cunard's finest and most famous liners.

RMS Queen Elizabeth & RMS Queen Mary passing each other mid-Atlantic

As it was now after 5PM, we headed back to our stateroom for a shower and to get dressed for dinner at 6.15PM. Dress code for that evening was formal and after a shower; we both donned a white shirt and bow tie, our suits and our black leather shoes. When we were ready, we headed back up to the Mauretania Restaurant on the upper deck and sat down at our table, eager to see what culinary delights were on tonight's menu.

I chose smoked salmon rose, garnished with Malossol sturgeon caviar and toast as a starter. The main course was pan-fried lemon sole with muniere butter, capers lemon and dill with a steamed fresh vegetable bouquet and parsley potatoes. Dessert was a delicious Marnier souffle with vanilla anglaise. I had never heard of – nor eaten – most of the items on the menu, but I thought, *"When on QE2, why not live a little!"* So I did and the meal was very enjoyable again.

Opposite the menu page were the dates on which members of the Royal Family had visited or sailed on the *QE2* throughout her 41 years of life.

HRH, the late Duke of Edinburgh had the distinction of being both the first and last royal visitor. On the 14th July 1967, he toured the uncompleted liner and he was due to make a visit on her last day in Britain on the 11th November 2008.

After dinner, we went exploring again. There really was so much to see. We started in the Midship Lobby, where we found that we had the lobby to ourselves. It was a good opportunity to take a few photographs of the lobby and I was impressed to see in a glass case the famous solid silver model of the *QE2* made by Asprey of London.

We then made our way to the Chart Room Bar and I was delighted to see a grand piano which had come from RMS *Queen Mary* – according to a brass plate which was attached below the piano's keyboard.

Behind the bar was a large decorative chart of the North Atlantic depicting *QE2*'s sailing routes east and west across the North Atlantic between Great

Solid Silver model of the QE2 made by Asprey of London

Author and Ian in the Chartroom Bar

Britain and the United States of America. I had seen pictures in books of a similar map on RMS *Queen Mary*, which was in the large restaurant on her "C" Deck; there were two miniature motorised models of the *Queen Mary* and the *Queen Elizabeth* attached to it: one sailing west and the other sailing east. Both depicted exactly where on their routes each liner was.

There were a wide variety of cocktails and much else on offer in the bar. I ordered a frozen banana daiquiri for us both. I had first tasted this cocktail many years ago in *Charlie Parker's*– a trendy cocktail bar in St Enoch's Square in Glasgow. I had always remembered the name of this cocktail and it was as enjoyable as I remembered it to be.

The next stop was to see the Grand Lounge which had – on the upper level – several shops; including Harrods, the Ocean Bookshop, a library and gift shop amongst many others.

Looking towards the stage of the Grand Lounge

On the lower deck of the Grand Lounge was the seating area in front of the stage. The stage had rich red velvet curtains hung across it, which were edged with a gold-coloured tassel fringe trim. The red chairs laid out around the floor in front of the stage, were the perfect complement to the curtains, giving the Grand Lounge a very warm and comfortable appearance.

From the Grand Lounge, we walked along the port side enclosed promenade deck and found ourselves back at The Golden Lion pub, which was handy as we had worked up a thirst. Ray Terry and his Jazz Band were setting up to play. We ordered drinks and sat down at a table and were very impressed with Ray and his Band. Ray was quite a character and everyone quickly warmed to his dry humour and excellent vocals. If you closed your eyes, you could be forgiven for thinking that the late, great vocalist, Mr Louis Armstrong was singing right in front of you.

We spent the evening at The Golden Lion and afterwards headed for bed at just after 11PM, feeling that the sea-air had knocked the two of us for six. On arriving back at our stateroom, we found two copies of the *Daily Programme* pushed underneath our door. This programme was delivered to our stateroom each night and informed us about the next day's events taking place all over the ship, as well as the navigational information for the following day.

Tomorrow's programme informed us that we were on a west by northerly course, following the great circle route across the North Atlantic Ocean, between Bishop Rock off the Scilly Isles, to the Grand Banks of Newfoundland in Canada.

We were both starting to feel a little bit peckish and considered trying to get a snack delivered to our room. "Do you think the kitchen will still be doing food at this time of night?" I asked Ian.

"There is only one way to find out!" he replied, picking up the telephone. Ian dialled the number for room service and ordered two cheese toasties and a pot of tea for two. Just a few minutes later there was a gentle knock on our door.

Ian opened the door and was greeted by a chap from the kitchen with a tray containing our late-night snack. There was even a smaller jug full of hot water in case we wanted a second cup of tea, plus a knife and fork each with two napkins.

"Wow! Now this is what I call room service," I said, taking a bite of my toastie, whilst Ian poured some tea for us. Ian nodded and commented on the excellent service which Cunard gave their passengers everywhere on the ship. "Now this is living!" I said taking another bite. It certainly was and you simply could not fault the level of service from the crew; no matter where you went on the QE2.

Once we had eaten our toasties and drank several cups of tea each, it was time to brush our teeth and call it a night. We each then got into our beds and quickly fell asleep.

CHAPTER 3

We go shopping on the Mezzanine Floor

Sunday, 12th October 2008

Weather: cloudy with a slightly choppy sea.

The first thing I did when I woke up, was to kneel on my bed and look out of the porthole to see if the sun was shining. Unfortunately, it was cloudy, but I was rewarded with a perfect view of *Queen Mary 2* directly in line with our porthole. *QM2* was off our port bow today and the waves around both liners were tipped with white foam.

After breakfast, we went for – what was becoming – an oft-repeated stroll around the Boat Decks. I must admit to never tiring of walking around the *QE2*. As we walked around the port and starboard Boat Decks, I could not help gazing above me at the davits: the crane-like devices which hold the

Our cat Rufus and the QM2

QM2 off QE2's portside bow

lifeboats in place and are used for supporting, raising, and lowering the lifeboats. I found myself thinking for the umpteenth time, "We are really here on the *QE2!*" At the risk of repeating myself: this experience certainly was a dream come true for me.

Even the outdoor swimming pool at the stern looked decidedly choppy today and was covered with a net to deter passengers from swimming in it. The two whirlpools which lay in front of the pool towards the stern were also empty. I decided to wait for a sunnier day; which hopefully would come soon enough and I would be able to go for a swim in the outdoor pool myself.

At the top of E Stairway on Boat Deck level, we came across the four tapestries depicting the *QE2's* launch which had been created by Helena Barynina Hernmarck.

The first tapestry showed a smiling Queen Elizabeth surrounded by dignitaries, waving up at the men on the portside bow as the newly

Two of the four Launch Tapestries by Helen Banynina Hernmarck

christened ship slid down the ways into the river Clyde. The next tapestry showed the men on the bow waving back at the Queen. The third tapestry depicted a similar view of the second tapestry and the fourth tapestry showed the QE2 floating on the Clyde, just in front of the mouth of the River Cart which flows into the Clyde almost opposite John Brown's Yard with RAF *736* Squadron flying over the new Cunarder in an anchor formation. It was probably no coincidence that this Squadron was used as *"736"* was the *QE2's* build number at Brown's Yard.

I wanted to buy some postcards to post whilst on board, so we headed for the Ocean Bookshop on the Mezzanine Floor, above the Grand Lounge to see what postcards they had for sale.

There were quite a few postcards to choose from; most had a photograph of the *QE2* on the front of each card, but I was amused by one which had a caricature drawing of the *QE2* leaping out of the ocean imitating a pod of dolphins in the sea in front of her. This was the one for me I thought, so I bought every one of the postcards with this drawing on them, which made a total of forty postcards. I was planning on sending a postcard to almost everyone whom we knew, telling them that we were on the *QE2*.

There were numerous *QE2* souvenirs for sale which we also bought that morning: Several *QE2* bookmarks; a black sweatshirt each – with the *QE2's* years of service to Cunard "1967 – 2008" on the front; various *QE2* pens; a couple of black-coloured padded pot-stand coasters, plus a pair of black padded oven gloves, all of which had *Queen Elizabeth 2* and the Cunard logo in gold on them and of course, a cotton tea towel with a drawing of the *QE2* on it.

We also bought two *Glencairn of Scotland* crystal whisky glasses; which had depictions of the *QE2* and the *QM2* in a circle on the outside of each glass. The words *"Final Tandem Crossing"* were etched on each glass at the top of the circle with the names of the two liners and the month and year of the voyage at the bottom of the circle. Both glasses were set in a smart blue box with a hinged lid which had the Cunard logo on the centre of the lid and *Glencairn*

Crystal of Scotland in the lower right-hand corner; both of which were in attractive gold lettering.

Outside the Ocean Bookshop, modelled on a mannequin, was a definite *"must-have"* for the both of us. Ian and I decided to buy it immediately when it went on sale on Tuesday 14th October. *The Final Tandem Crossing T-shirt* which had a print of the *QE2* and the *QM2* on the back, with the famous Manhattan skyline dominated by the Empire State Building, the Statue of Liberty and the Chrysler Building behind both liners. Underneath the two ships was the anticipated date of our arrival in New York on 16th October 2008. On the front left-hand breast side of the t-shirt, was a small print of the two liners set in a small gold circle, again with the liner's names and our date of arrival in New York.

I was very thankful that we had borrowed a large suitcase from our friend Christine to add to the two large *Antler* suitcases which we had brought with us. I had guessed that we would be going home with a lot more than we had started out with.

After our shopping spree, we went to the Yacht Club Bar which overlooked the stern. Using one of the *QE2* pens which I had bought earlier, I started to write some of the postcards. This pen had a small model of the *QE2* floating in clear liquid in the clear top half of the pen. The Statue of Liberty and the Chrysler Building were at one end of the top part of the pen with Big Ben and the dome of St Paul's Cathedral in London at the opposite end. The *QE2* "sailed" between the two ends of the pen – depending on which way you held it.

I wrote about 15 postcards that morning and after lunch, we went back to the Yacht Club and I wrote another 20 cards. All this time, I was still on my quest to find the builder's plate. However, I was not any closer to finding it, despite my continual questions to various members of the crew; asking if they knew where it was.

Although I have always been an optimist; I was beginning to wonder if there actually was such an item on board. I was starting to have serious doubts as

Model of RMS Britannia outside the Yacht Club Bar

Yacht Club Entrance

to whether or not I would find the builder's plate for the *QE2*. Surely if there was a builder's plate, *someone* would know where it was? So far, not one crew member had even heard of it, which worried me a little. We still had three full days at sea before we arrived in New York; hopefully by then, I would have met a crew member who would know: A. What I was talking about and B. Where the *QE2*'s builder's plate was located.

We headed back to our stateroom to shower and get changed for tonight's evening meal which was another formal dress affair. We were now getting quite used to "dressing for dinner" and enjoyed donning suits, white shirts and bow ties every evening, not forgetting our polished black shoes. It all added to the occasion in what was such a grand setting.

When we were ready, we made our way up to the Mauretania Restaurant. Once more our pleasant waiters and waitress were waiting for us and escorted us to our table. The menu for this evening's meal had a splendid picture of the *QE2* on the front of the menu card – as seen through the scaffolding at John Brown's shipyard in Clydebank. This scaffolding would eventually become the launch platform which would send the new Cunarder down into the river Clyde.

Inside the menu; there were a host of interesting facts about *QE2*'s launch:

The gold scissors which the HM the Queen had used to cut the ribbon which released the bottle of wine which smashed onto the side of the newly-named liner, were the same scissors which her mother had used to launch RMS *Queen Elizabeth* in 1938 and her grandmother had also used to launch RMS *Queen Mary* in 1934.

I did not know that and became engrossed in reading more.

Apparently, after the Queen had pressed the button which electronically released the launching trigger – nothing happened and the ship did not move. Workmen high up on the deck of the new Cunarder leaned over the railings and shouted, 'Give us a shove!' The Shipyard Director, George Parker, obligingly went over to the bows and pushed. By coincidence, the ship began to move down the slipway into the river Clyde. It was a little over two minutes since the Queen had named the ship, before she slid into the waters of the Clyde.

I remember watching the launch on a TV in the main hall at my primary school and vividly remember this anxious delay.

Other details included; the considerable weight of the ten bundles of drag links on either side of the ship which were used to steady the ship on her journey into the river. Each bundle of drag links weighed over 70 tonnes and meant that the *QE2* slid down the slipway at over 18mph.

On board the empty ship, there were 150 men with another 161 onshore, all to make certain that it was a smooth launch.

I read all these very interesting details and then remembered that my waitress was waiting patiently at my side to take my order. "I'm so sorry," I apologised to her. "This is all such interesting reading!"

I turned my gaze onto the right-hand page of the menu and saw that tonight's dinner was called, the "*Historic RMS Queen Elizabeth Dinner Menu*." I guessed that this menu had been offered on the first *Queen Elizabeth*. For starters: I had chicken broth with matzo balls, followed by fresh Scottish salmon poached in a court bouillon on sautéed leaf spinach, boiled potatoes and chive hollandaise. Dessert was called "Dome of Grand Marnier Mousse with Marinated Oranges." I wrote in my diary that night: "This was the best dinner so far!"

As I write this, my mouth is watering at the memory of this very tasty meal. I had never tasted such delicious food. I asked the waiters to convey my highest compliments to the chefs. My compliments were also due to Cunard, for ensuring that their passengers had such memorable and delicious meals to eat and enjoy each evening.

After this lovely meal, we went to The Golden Lion pub, where we had a few drinks before Ray Terry and his band began entertaining us for an hour or so.

Then Jenny; the hostess, took the microphone and ably assisted by a chap called Kennedy, announced that it was time to "throw our inhibitions overboard." The karaoke was about to begin. One of the first couples to get up and sing was a man and woman dressed like Sonny and Cher – complete with wigs and sixties clothes – who provided a lot of laughs with their rendition of "*I've Got You Babe.*"

Never one to miss an opportunity to sing in front of people, Ian filled out the yellow slip of paper – which was on every table in the pub – with his name and choice of song; which was The Walker Brothers' "*You've Lost That Loving Feeling.*" He has a very good strong voice and drew cheers and applause from the audience when he had finished singing.

When the karaoke night ended, we made our way to the Yacht Club Bar which was by now, very busy. We sat down beside a pleasant couple who introduced themselves to us as "Diane from Brooklyn, New York" and her friend Malcolm from London. We started chatting to them and I was very impressed when Diane told us that this was her *eighth* time on the *QE2*. We spent a few hours talking and drinking with the two of them, before calling it a night and heading back to our stateroom and bed.

CHAPTER 4

We meet Captain McNaught

Monday, 13th October 2008

Weather: cloudy with sunny intervals and a
cool breeze, slight swell in the sea.

This morning I rose early and decided to go for a swim in the indoor swimming pool down on Seven Deck, which was the lowest deck on board which was open to passengers. "I'll meet some new crew members down here," I thought to myself, "Perhaps one of them will have heard of the builder's plate."

Unfortunately, no one had. Undeterred I resolved to keep asking. Before my swim, I had a workout in the gym which was next door to the indoor pool. After my workout, I stepped down into the pool – via the steps at the side of the pool.

I had two surprises. Firstly, the water was not as warm as I had been expecting and secondly, the water was salty.

"I bet I know where the crew got this water from!" I said to myself, realising that I was probably swimming in North Atlantic seawater. "I never thought I'd be swimming this far out at sea – almost in the middle of the North Atlantic!"

After my swim, I met up with Ian and we went for breakfast in the Mauretania Restaurant which had become the daily norm whilst on board. After breakfast, we went for our first walk of the day around the Boat Decks. *Queen Mary 2* was off the starboard bow today, gleaming in the bright sunshine. It was rather windy as we walked along the port and starboard Boat Decks and we decided to take a break from the wind and sat in the deck seats behind the Sports Centre area.

This position gave us a good view overlooking the outside lido decking seating area with sun loungers stretched from one side of the ship to the other. It also gave us a good view of the stern. The loungers were empty this morning – no doubt due to the brisk breeze which was blowing across the deck.

It was announced over the ship's tannoy at midday, that the *QE2* had crossed over the midway point of our voyage across the Atlantic. The distance between Southampton and New York is 3,632 nautical miles, which is equivalent to 4,179.6 miles. It meant we had sailed 2,089.8 miles since we had left Southampton.

During lunch, word quickly spread amongst the passengers who were there, to lookout of the starboard windows at *Queen Mary 2*. "Look at the rainbow over *Queen Mary 2!*" someone said. All eyes turned to the starboard windows to gaze upon the *QM2*.

Sure enough; there was a large rainbow neatly framing the *QM2* from bow to stern. The rainbow had chosen to begin at *QM2*'s bow and end precisely at her stern which was rather miraculous to witness. As luck would have it, neither

Ian nor I had either a camera or video camera with us, so we had to be content with just seeing this unusual occurrence and storing it in our memories.

After an enjoyable post-lunch stroll around the Boat Decks – which had become another custom – we reached the Boat Deck behind the Sports Centre. This gave us an opportunity to see what was there. The Sports Centre had an enclosed deck-tennis court; a net for driving golf balls into, as well as a putting green and two shuffleboard courts.

The sun shone down strongly and the seawater of the *QE2*'s wake churned a deep blue; fading into the far distance behind us in an easterly direction. "Great Britain is that way!" I said to Ian, pointing in the easterly direction of the *QE2*'s wake.

That afternoon we went to the Funnel Bar and treated ourselves to the famous very tasty – and most enjoyable – *Cunard Cream Tea*. This consisted of a cup of tea, a neatly cut chicken and cucumber sandwich – with the crusts removed, plus a delicious sultana scone filled with cream for each of us. It certainly was as tasty and enjoyable as I expected it to be; having read about *Cunard's Cream Teas* in the many books I have at home on Cunard's liners.

Whilst we sat there, we were joined by a man who lived in Clydebank no-less. He told us that he lived a stone's throw away from what *had* been John Brown's shipyard. He went on to say that only the slipway on which the *Queens Mary* and *Elizabeth* and the *QE2* herself, had slid down into the river Clyde, the 150-tonnes Titan Crane on the left – as viewed from the river – and the Fitting-Out Basin, were all that remained of the shipyard. I *had* intended to visit John Brown's shipyard on my next visit home to Scotland – armed with my video camera – but sadly, on hearing this bad news – that was now never going to happen.

All the buildings of John Brown's shipyard had been demolished. This was very sad news in my opinion, considering all the famous liners and well-known Royal Navy vessels which had been built there.

When we finished our cream teas, we went back to our stateroom to shower and change into our formal attire. For – on *this* evening – guests in the Mauretania Restaurant on an early sitting, were invited to meet Captain McNaught and his officers for cocktails in the Queen's Room which was on the Quarter Deck, between 5.45PM until 6.30PM.

It was very busy when we arrived and everyone was offered a complimentary glass of champagne – which seemed to be in permanent supply on this voyage. We joined the long queue to meet Captain McNaught. Finally, after a good few minute's wait, we were ushered over to meet him and to have our photograph taken with the Captain.

Captain McNaught had a firm handshake – which always impresses me when I meet someone new – as it is usually a sign of their good character. He had a warm and friendly nature and came across as a very nice man. He asked us if we were enjoying the voyage and we answered, "Yes – very much!" The photographer then asked us to stand beside Captain McNaught and he

Captain McNaught, the author and Ian. Photo courtesy of Cunard

then took our photograph and that was it. We walked away to let the couple behind us step forward and meet Captain McNaught.

As he obviously had a lot of other passengers to meet and get photographed with, we moved on and all my plans of telling Captain McNaught of how I first saw the *QE2* in John Brown's Fitting-Out Basin, four days after the Queen had launched her when I was six years old and also how I had briefly worked in his home town of Sunderland a few years previously, all which went out of the window, or perhaps I should say – given the location– overboard!

I just dried up and felt that with so many other passengers for Captain McNaught to meet and get photographed with, he did not have time for small talk. Still – at least we got to meet and shake hands with the Captain of the *QE2*. After this occasion and as we headed to our restaurant, we came across another great photo opportunity.

A large cloth screen backdrop had been set up outside the Queen's Room and printed on the screen was the Grand Staircase from the White Star liners *Titanic* and *Olympic*. This staircase featured memorably, in the James Cameron blockbuster film *Titanic*. We *had* to get our photograph taken in front of this – well – quite a few photographs actually! We were told that these photographs and the one with Captain McNaught would be available here, for us to purchase the following day.

Feeling rather grand and pleased with ourselves after these very memorable photographs, we headed to the Mauretania Restaurant for that evening's dinner. "I wonder what's on tonight's menu card?" I said to Ian. I did not mean the food menu; I meant what historical information would be printed on the menu card opposite the food choices. On the front of the menu card was the first logo for the *QE2*: a large red capital "*E*" next to an equally large red number "*2*". When viewed – the "*E*" and "*2*" side by side like this, it gave the impression of forming a "*Q*". This logo was widely used for advertising the *QE2* in the 1960's.

Inside the menu card were the details of *what* the new liner *might* be called before her launch and the betting odds, which came from a betting shop in

The author and Ian in front of the Olympic & Titanic's
"Grand Staircase". Photo courtesy of Cunard

Glasgow for each name. Two former Cunard liners names were included in the list: *Aquitania* at odds of 10-1 and *Mauretania* at 12-1, as well as the names of most members of the Queen's immediate family. Winston Churchill; John F. Kennedy and the recently deceased land-speed record holder, Scotsman Donald Campbell were other suggestions featured, amongst a few others. *Queen Elizabeth* was Cunard's name-choice for the new liner.

After her launch, the chairman of Cunard at that time, Sir Basil Smallpeice, proposed the use of the Arabic "2" after the Queen's name and the matter was settled and thus the new liner became known and loved the world over as the *Queen Elizabeth 2* or *QE2* for short.

Having quickly read all this, I turned my attention to the food menu. I chose barley vegetable broth with ginger croutons; followed by pan-fried fillet of cod, parsley lemon butter sauce with crisp bacon, French-style green peas and sautéed Yukon gold potatoes. For dessert, I had a treacle tart with butterscotch topping and vanilla ice cream. It was yet another very tasty and enjoyable meal.

After we had eaten, we went to The Golden Lion pub for a few drinks, whilst we listened to and enjoyed Ray Terry and his Band. As the Pursers Office was open 24 hours, I thought that I would take advantage of this fact and make sure that I posted off the postcards which I had already written. We went to collect the cards from our stateroom and then went up to the Purser's Office, which was located on Two Deck.

Ian and I were greeted at the Purser's Office by Darryl, a friendly Australian chap. I told him that I wanted to send "a few postcards" and I took the thick batch of postcards from the inner breast pocket of my suit jacket and placed them on the countertop.

"Wow!" he exclaimed. "How many do you have?"

"There are 35 here," I said. "I still have a few more to write."

"That's a record!" he said. "I've never seen a passenger post so many postcards on board!" He told us that the most postcards he had seen a passenger post onboard was 16. He laughed when I told him that I wanted almost everyone whom we knew, to know that Ian and I were on the *QE2*.

Darryl carefully stamped each postcard with a rubber stamp which read *"Posted on the QE2"* above a print of the *QE2* as viewed from her starboard side. After he had stamped each card, I took the opportunity to ask Darryl if he had heard of the builder's plate, or if he knew where it was? He did not know, which did not surprise me.

I was pleased that the bulk of my postcards had now been posted and resolved to write the remaining ones in the next few days before we arrived in New York. We left the Purser's Office and made our way to the Yacht Club Bar for the *ABBA Tribute Party* hosted by the resident DJ Gary King and the cruise staff.

There was an *ABBA Special* on at the Yacht Club this evening and on our arrival, we sat down at a table next to the couple whom we had met the previous night: Diane from Brooklyn and her friend Malcolm from London. We ordered a round of drinks for us all and the Yacht Club quickly filled up. Then at 11:30 PM, the DJ started playing ABBA records, which soon had the dancefloor very busy.

After Ian and I had a couple of drinks, we squeezed our way onto the dancefloor and joined in the dancing. The DJ had started playing "*Dancing Queen*" – which seemed very appropriate for the *QE2* at that moment – with all the dancefloor activity.

Whilst we were dancing, a dark-haired chap came up to us and asked if he could join us.

"Certainly!" I said to him and obligingly moved over to let him dance beside Ian and I.

After about four records, we made our way back to our table for a drink. "It's *very* hot on the dancefloor!" I said to Diane and Malcolm as we sat down.

As I took my seat, I noticed a chap sit down at a nearby table and wipe his head and face which was soaking with sweat. He was in full Scottish dress and he was wearing a green-over-grey tartan kilt complete with sporran and jacket. He had a huge grin on his face and was one of a group of men who were all dressed in kilts and obviously enjoying themselves immensely. I smiled sympathetically towards him – as we know from experience at a friend's wedding a few years previously – how hot you can get dancing, when dressed in full Scottish regalia.

The evening was a great success and it certainly was a good party. When we arrived back in our stateroom that night we made and drank a pot of tea before heading for bed.

Our cabin steward had thoughtfully turned down our beds – as he did every evening. He also left a foil-wrapped chocolate for each of us in a little China dish which sat on the dresser between our beds each night. This was a nightly tradition for passengers, which I had read took place on Cunard liners in the past and was another example of the thoughtful customer service which Cunard seemed to excel at.

I closed my eyes and thought about the events of the day and it suddenly struck me that I had missed a good opportunity to find out if the *QE2 did* have a builder's plate and, if so, where it *was*.

"I should have asked Captain McNaught where the builders plate is," I said to Ian.

"I didn't think of that myself," he replied. "We didn't have long with him and there were so many people waiting behind us to meet him."

"It didn't even cross my mind," I said, annoyed with myself for not thinking of asking the Captain where the builder's plate was. If any crew member knew the whereabouts of the builder's plate, the *QE2*'s Captain was bound to have known.

We only had two more full days at sea before we docked in New York, early on Thursday morning. "Time is running out," I said to Ian, with a hint of anxiety in my voice.

"We'll see what we can find out tomorrow," Ian answered and yawned loudly.

"I don't know who else we could ask," I said. "Everyone we have asked so far doesn't seem to know what we're talking about."

"There has to be someone on board who'll help us find it," said Ian.

"I hope so," I replied. "I really do." On that note, I rolled over and went to sleep.

CHAPTER 5

Sunbathing at the Funnel Bar

Tuesday, 14th October 2008

Weather: Cloudy with long sunny periods and some strong afternoon sunshine. Sea calm

---

We awoke to cloudy skies but with some strong sunshine breaking through. *Queen Mary 2* was sailing off our port bow. To be more precise, she was sailing immediately opposite our porthole again, which was very considerate of her.

After breakfast, we went for our first walk of the day around the Boat Decks. Whilst we walked down the starboard steps from the forward Sun Deck, Ian took a good photograph of the *QE2*'s funnel emitting a hazy, black cloud which was emitting from her nine diesel engines far below.

"Changed days!" I thought to myself, looking at her funnel. Thinking of how in days gone by, steamers were well-known for pumping out thick black smoke from their funnels, especially in the days when they burnt coal.

Looking down onto starboard Boat Deck from forward Sun Deck steps

We went back inside to the shopping area to buy the remainder of the presents which we wanted to take home for our friends. More importantly, to buy the *Final Tandem* T-shirts which we had seen on the mannequin in the Gift Shop a few days ago and which had gone on sale this morning.

The T-shirts had sold out in the gift shop by the time we had arrived, but someone told us that they were also on sale in the duty-free liquor shop. So, we headed off there – where there were still some T-shirts left and we bought one each. That was a big relief!

After securing this all-important purchase, I left Ian to try his luck in the casino on the upper deck, whilst I made my way to the theatre which was on the same deck – for today's *Enrichment Lecture*.

Today's speaker was Mr Bill Miller, the well-known international authority about the great ocean liners. He gave a very interesting talk, although I only learnt one new fact. He said that Cunard had briefly considered naming their new liner after Diana, the Princess of Wales, when they were planning *Queen Mary 2* in 1990.

Afterwards, I met up with Ian, who unfortunately did not win anything but nevertheless he had enjoyed the experience. On the way to the Funnel Bar for lunch, we watched a pod of young whales swim by off the starboard side. We reached the Quarter Deck – or *Helideck* as the crew called it – just above the stern, where I was able to film *QE2*'s wake, which stretched out far behind us in an easterly direction, before fading into the distance. The sky was now clearing and the sun beat down upon us.

Arriving at the Funnel Bar a few minutes before midday, we positioned ourselves near the starboard side. We stood underneath a small speaker, which was part of the ship's tannoy system, to listen to – and record on my video camera – today's navigational briefing from one of the two Bridge Third Officers.

View of the stern from the aft Quarter Deck

Today's briefing disclosed some very interesting news – for want of a more respectful phrase. "At 10:30AM this morning; *QE2* was 275 nautical miles north of the resting place on the seabed of the *Titanic.*" The Third Officer continued, "This position was as close as we got to the ill-fated liner." I said a quiet prayer for the many souls who lost their lives on that fateful night.

After hearing this news, we walked quietly over to the serving area of the Funnel Bar and ordered our lunch before sitting down on two of the sun-loungers.

We had an enjoyable lunch in the Funnel Bar of baked potatoes with sour crème with bacon and cheese. As the sky had now cleared of clouds completely, we decided that after lunch, we would take advantage of the brilliant sunshine and do a spot of sunbathing, with the funnel rising majestically in front of us.

Funnel Bar

I went to the bar to buy a couple of drinks for us to enjoy on our loungers, and on my return to Ian, I started chatting to a friendly young woman who had been talking to him. Her name was Laura and she said she lived in Washington. She did not say – and I did not ask her – whether it was the city of that name or the State. We shared stories about what a thrill it was being on the *QE2* and at the end of our brief chat, she asked me if she could hug me – as my excitement of being on the *QE2* "*just oozed*" from me.

"Of course, you can hug me!" I said to her and gave her a big hug. She thanked me very much, then went on her way and we never saw each other again. But I am sure, that like me, she remembers our brief happy meeting on the *QE2*.

The sun was still shining down on us when, over the ship tannoy system, came the announcement that in a few minutes we were going to have a flypast from a Canadian Fisheries Protection Task Force aircraft. Shortly after this, a low-flying jet flew between us and *QM2*. The jet went by both liners at a terrific speed and served as an indication of our approach to land – after four days alone at sea.

Ian went over to the bar and came back with two glasses of liquid – which looked *very* familiar to me. "That's not what I think it is?" I said to him, taking hold of one glass.

"Taste it and see!" Ian said with a smile.

I took a sip which confirmed my suspicions. "*Irn-Bru!*" I exclaimed – this soft drink – as every Scotsman, Scottish woman or Scottish child knows – is often called "*Scotland's other national drink.*"

I took another sip and said to Ian. "Well, – I didn't expect to find *Irn-Bru* on the *QE2*."

"She has everything else," said Ian.

"True!" I agreed. "Still, I didn't expect *this*!" As we sipped this most welcome soft drink, the sun disappeared and a strong breeze blew around the Funnel

Bar. We decided against doing anymore sunbathing at this time and instead, walked around the starboard Boat Deck. At this point, with the sun not making another appearance, it turned decidedly chilly with the breeze blowing stronger across the deck.

We watched another pod of whales swim by, spouting from their blowholes again and after staring at the sea for a while, we got tired of watching to see more whales. We crossed over to the portside Boat Deck and strolled underneath the lifeboats. We paused to photograph a blue sign on the superstructure wall, which was just before the steps which led up to the forward Sun Deck. The sign informed us that walking five times around the Boat Decks is the equivalent to one mile.

"I've lost count of how many miles we must have walked so far on this voyage," I said to Ian, nodding to the sign.

"Quite a few," he replied.

We climbed up the steps to the forward Sun Deck, pausing at the top of the stairs to admire the mast, which I had recently learnt, had been cut out of aluminium by the late Mr Arthur Douglass who had worked at John Brown's shipyard at the time of *QE2*'s construction. The mast was then fitted onto the *QE2* about a year later.

I had been told this by his son; Eric Douglass, from whom I had bought an invitation card to *QE2*'s launch on *eBay* a few months before our voyage. Eric also told me that the cards were supposed to be handed in at the gate to Brown's Yard on the day of her launch, but that he had asked the man on the gate if he could keep his invitation card. As Eric was then a young eleven-year-old boy, the man on the gate nodded and said he could. I am glad he did because the *QE2*'s launch ticket is now amongst my Cunardia treasures at home.

Up on the Sun Deck, we looked down at the bow and the sea was very calm all around the *QE2*. The United States were approximately 900 miles ahead of us

Portside view of QE2's mast

View from forward Sun Deck of QE2's bow

The author enjoying a seat amidships on the starboard Boat Deck

– we had been told this earlier that afternoon, when the *QE2*'s tannoy system gave our daily position at midday.

We walked across the Sun Deck, down the starboard steps and along the length of the starboard Boat Deck, noting that the davits on the starboard side of the *QE2*, had lifeboats with odd numbers painted on them, whilst the even-numbered lifeboats were on the portside.

When we reached the aft-quarter deck, near *QE2*'s stern. Another pod of whales were making their presence known by breaking the surface of the ocean and sending more jets into the air. The whales were swimming by us in an easterly direction. There must have been about half a dozen whales at least and we and a few other passengers spotted at least 10 sprays into the air at various times in the sea as they swam by the *QE2*. We spent another 10 minutes or so watching for whales but we did not see any more and as time was marching on, we decided to go back to our stateroom for a shower and get dressed for dinner.

Tonight, the Mauretania Restaurant had been decorated with many flags hanging around the entire ceiling from countries right across the world. These flags were a demonstration of how international the *QE2's* crew was – usually around 50 nationalities and just how well-travelled the *QE2* herself was. This evening was a traditional event which occurred on every voyage; usually on the last evening in which formal dress was required and was known as the "*Baked Alaska Parade.*"

Our waiting staff ushered us to our seats and presented each of us with a menu for that evening's meal. On the front of the menu was an aerial photograph of the *QE2* leaving Southampton Water, loaded up with troops and equipment to liberate the Falkland Islands in May 1982.

The heading below this picture read: "*A Queen Goes to War.*" Inside; was a detailed explanation of her 6,796-mile voyage to South Georgia in the Falklands and then back home to Southampton. On the opposite page were the menu choices for what was billed as "*Captain McNaught's Farewell Dinner.*"

Once the starters and main course had been eaten, the serving staff were joined by the kitchen chefs and they all proceeded to serve the *Baked Alaska* dessert; which is a dessert consisting of ice cream and cake topped with browned meringue.

As the main lights in the restaurant had been dimmed for that evening; the waitresses, waiters and chefs "paraded" around the tables, holding Roman Candles, and serving the delicious Baked Alaska dessert. It certainly was a colourful and glittering occasion. We had eaten many exquisite dishes over the last four evenings and tonight's meal and the memories of each delicious evening meal will stay with us forever. We had never before, tasted such well-prepared food. After dinner, we called in at The Golden Lion pub to wash down our meal.

Ray Terry and his bandmates were performing there as usual, for the first part of the evening and at the end of their set, Jenny took hold of the microphone and announced the final karaoke session to be held on the *QE2's* final westbound crossing of the North Atlantic Ocean. "I've got to enter this," said

Ian, writing his name and song choice again onto the yellow slip of paper on our table.

"Which song are you going to sing?" I asked him.

"It's a surprise!" he answered mischievously. I shook my head and left it at that. I knew that whichever song he sang, he would sing it well. I waited to see if Jenny would ask him to sing for that evening's guests.

As it turned out; almost everyone who was in The Golden Lion that evening wanted to get up and sing. After some very good singers had sung their song-choice, Jenny announced that they would have one final song – and she called Ian's name.

Ian walked onto the floor and took the microphone which she offered to him and sang Elton John's *"Don't Let the Sun Go Down on Me."*

"Good choice," I said to myself. I had heard him sing this song before and he always made an excellent job of it. The crowd cheered and clapped for him at the end of the song and he came off the floor with a modest grin on his face.

"Well done!" I said, patting his shoulder, when he came back to where I was standing at the front of the bar of The Golden Lion.

Jenny then announced that the karaoke was over for the night. "That's a claim to fame for you," I said to Ian. "Singing the *last* karaoke song on the *QE2*'s final westbound crossing!" Ian smiled and looked relieved that it was over.

"Let us go to the Yacht Club now," I said. "You look like you could do with a *stiff* drink." Ian nodded and we made our way to the Yacht Club, which was busy again tonight. Eventually, we made our way to the bar and ordered a *Canadian Club* each: This is a Canadian rye whisky, mixed with ginger ale and a lot of ice. We decided to call it a night after downing our drinks – as we had all our packing to do before we disembarked in New York on Thursday morning.

We got back to our stateroom and just before I got into my bed, I opened the curtains over the porthole. "What are you doing?" asked Ian.

"Just checking that *Queen Mary 2* is still there," I said. She was. I could see a blaze of lights in the distance, it was an impressive sight to see. "She's still up and partying!" I said to Ian.

With that, I closed the curtains and got into my bed. "Time is running out for me to find the builder's plate before we dock in New York; the day after tomorrow."

There was no reply from Ian as he was already asleep. "Help me to find the builder's plate, Saint Anthony please," I murmured as I got into my bed. As a child, I had been taught by my Mum, that Saint Anthony was the Patron Saint of Lost Items and frequently "lost items" turned up after asking for his help to find them. They still do!

CHAPTER 6

Our last full day at sea

Wednesday, 15th October 2008

Weather: cloudy, after a very sunny start to the day. Very smooth and calm sea

---

I had set the alarm on my mobile phone for 6:30AM, as I wanted to have a swim in the outdoor pool today. Also, the man from Clydebank whom we had met in the Funnel Bar on Monday afternoon, had recommended an early morning soak in one of the two whirlpools – weather and sea conditions permitting of course.

We arrived at the stern just before seven and just as the sun began rising from behind a few clouds which were in the eastern sky behind the *QE2*.

No one was in either of the whirlpools so we walked over to the whirlpool on the portside. "I'll have a swim first," I said to Ian, nodding towards the swimming pool which was in front of the whirlpools. The swimming pool was also empty.

"Okay," he answered. "I'll get into the whirlpool as it will be warmer in there."

Early morning sunrise on Quarter and Upper Decks

I lowered myself into the pool using the steps at the side of the swimming pool and swam a few lengths. The water in the pool slapped rather heavily against each side of the pool and could best be described – once again – as a bit "choppy." After a couple more lengths of the pool, I climbed out and joined Ian in the whirlpool. "It is a lot warmer in here," I remarked as I sank into the whirlpool. "The water in the swimming pool was a *wee* bit chilly."

I stretched out and enjoyed the much warmer water of the whirlpool. The sun was climbing higher into the sky from behind the collection of rosy-red clouds in the eastern sky and it soon lit up the sea and the stern and aft decks of the *QE2*.

From this position on the stern deck; we had a good view of the two cranes which faced each other at either side of the stern. Sitting in the whirlpool, which was in front of the stern railings, I had a good opportunity to look more closely at these two cranes. I discovered later, that these cranes were known as "Two Deck Aft Mooring Deck Cranes" and they were to be used for lowering life rafts for the crew in the unfortunate event of extreme danger occurring to the ship. The inflatable life rafts were stored in white drums which lay in-between the cranes. Thankfully; to my knowledge, these life rafts had *never* been used.

A few passengers had joined us on the stern deck and were also enjoying the beautiful sunrise. The *QM2* was off our starboard bow this morning, sailing gracefully towards our joint destination of New York.

We dried ourselves and, as it was a little bit cold wearing just our swimming trunks, we both put on tracksuit bottoms and a sweatshirt each and decided to see if the Mauretania Restaurant was open for breakfast. We made our way back inside via the double door at the rear starboard side of the Yacht Club. We paused to take a few photographs, looking at the outside of the Yacht Club and the pool on One Deck, as well as the aft superstructure of the ship, which were all glowing brightly courtesy of the early morning rising sun.

Large model of RMS Mauretania near the top of D stairway

Just outside, near the top of D Stairway and before we entered the restaurant, we discovered a very large model of RMS *Mauretania*, looking splendid in a glass case. A smaller model of RMS *Mauretania* was to be found at the aft end of the restaurant, behind a row of chairs with highly-polished oak wooden arms and covered in a pleasant light blue material.

All was quiet in the restaurant and there was not a soul to be seen – not even the waiting staff. All the tables had been neatly laid – probably after the second dinner sitting last night – ready for this morning's breakfast. As breakfast did not start until 08:00AM, this was a good opportunity to film the entire Mauretania Restaurant.

After breakfast and our first daily stroll around the Boat Decks, we decided that we had better start packing our suitcases. It gave us both a sad feeling realising that our voyage on the *QE2* was ending the next day and I was worried that I had yet to find the builder's plate. Neither of us had ever been to New York before, so that thought cheered us up a little.

White Horses sculpture by Anthea Wynne in Mauretania Restaurant

Smaller model of RMS Mauretania – aft end of Mauretania Restaurant

We packed most of our clothes into our suitcases – as well as the considerable number of gifts which we had bought. Once we had finished packing, we went to *QE2*'s spa, as we had booked, what turned out to be – a most relaxing seaweed body wrap and massage from a friendly young Australian woman who was the massage therapist. Her name was Brodie.

Inside the spa, two tables were both covered with a large sheet of aluminium foil which hung down almost to the floor on either side of the massage tables. Ian and I each lay down on a table. Brodie had a large plastic bowl in her hands, which contained a green paste made from seaweed and using a flat spatula-like implement, proceeded to smear our entire bodies with the paste. This would apparently draw out any toxins which were present in our skin.

After Brodie had covered both our bodies in the seaweed paste, she wrapped the large sheet of foil over each of us. She then placed a couple of heavy blankets on top of us and left us to "*cook*" – as she termed it. Brodie then excused herself and informed us that she would be back in about half an hour.

It was very relaxing wrapped in the foil sheet and heavy blankets and I think we both dozed off for a while. When Brodie returned, she woke us up and invited us to both take a shower to wash off the seaweed paste. After we each had a shower, we returned to the massage tables and then she gave each of us a very thorough massage, after which we both felt very relaxed and very clean.

We left the spa and got into the lift up to One Deck. From there, we walked around the ship until we found ourselves again at the Funnel Bar just in time to hear the sailing plan for the following morning of our New York arrival over the ship's tannoy system: "The New York Port Authority has given the *QE2* permission to sail up the Hudson River to her New York home at Pier 90 in Manhattan," announced one of the *QE2*'s Third Officers – who took it turn with the other Bridge Third Officer to give the daily announcements over the ship's tannoy system.

In fact, I already knew this. Before we sailed, I had received a letter from Cunard, informing me that the *QE2* was going to be allowed to sail *up* the Hudson River, as this was to be *QE2*'s final arrival in New York. The *QM2* and all other liners were now required to dock at the recently completed Docking Terminal in Brooklyn.

According to the information relayed over the tannoy, we would pass the Ambrose Tower at 4:00AM; *QE2* was then to sail under the Verrazano Bridge at 4:40AM and pass the Statue of Liberty at 5:00AM. A high tide was forecast for the following morning which helped facilitate this approach into Manhattan.

We were pleased to hear that the Statue of Liberty would be on *QE2*'s portside. Our stateroom was on the portside of *QE2*, so we would be able to see the Statue of Liberty from our porthole if we chose. The *QE2* would then sail to Pier 90 in Manhattan, arriving at 6:00AM.

From the indoor swimming pool down on Deck 7, to the bookshop up on Quarter Deck, from the Mauritania Restaurant to the Yacht Club Bar and The Golden Lion Pub, I had asked every member of the crew whom I had met. But everyone I asked, did not know where the builder's plate was – and most had not even heard of it. A crew member I had spoken to about it suggested I talk to "*Tommy*" in the engine room – "as he has been on the ship for over 20 years." But "*Tommy*" was proving a difficult man to find.

I was not having any luck at all in finding the builder's plate and on what was our fifth and final full day at sea, I was resigned to *not* finding it.

After a morning of "*I don't know*" from all the crew members whom I had met from the stern to the bow, I was feeling less and less hopeful that I would find the *QE2*'s builder's plate.

However, at lunchtime as we walked into the Mauretania Restaurant from a different entrance to the one which we had normally used, i.e., not the entrance amidships by the lifts, but at the bow end of the Mauretania Restaurant, we met a chap called Marius. He sat behind a desk at this entrance to the restaurant. Marius was the Maître d' of the Mauretania Restaurant. After saying hello and briefly chatting to him, I trudged rather despondently to our table.

Ian stayed behind and asked Marius if *he* knew where the builder's plate was on the ship. Marius replied saying that it might be up on the walls around the Officers' Ward Room, where there is a framed plaque from every port which the *QE2* has visited.

Ian asked him if it was possible to get into the Ward Room – wherever it was – to have a look. Marius told Ian, "The Ward Room is for officers only." But then he said, "Passengers *are* allowed in by invitation only."

"That's a pity that we can't get in to have a look," said Ian pointing to me. "It would really make his voyage if he could see the builder's plate."

"In that case," said Marius. "I invite you both to see the Officers' Ward Room." Ian arranged for us to meet Marius after lunch and he quickly came over to join me at our table and share this good news with me. My spirits lifted and I felt very hopeful that we *would* find QE2's builder's plate in the Officers Ward Room and so I quickly ate my lunch. I could not explain why, but suddenly I had a very good feeling that my search for the *QE2's* builder's plate was about to pay off.

After we had finished our lunch, we followed Marius up to the Officers Ward Room and were surprised to see that *this* room was located on the immediate right-hand side of the lift door which we had used a few times, to go up to the Mauritania Restaurant from our stateroom. We had been passing it all this time!

We followed Marius into the room and he pointed out the plaques which lined the top of every wall in the room. These plaques were too small to be the builder's plate I thought, looking all around the room. As I glanced around the room, out of the corner of my eye on the wall behind me on my right-hand side, I noticed a large silver sign on the wall with the word "Clydebank" on it.

I hurried over to the sign for a closer look and there it was! *The QE2's builder's plate!*

"*I've found it at last!*" I said triumphantly.

The builder's plate was high up on the back wall of the Ward Room, in-between two large coloured photographs of HM The Queen and HRH Prince Phillip. Below it, hanging from a highly-polished wooden stand was the huge ship's bell from RMS *Aquitania.*

This bell was made from brass and "*Aquitania*" was stamped in an arc formation in capital letters, just below the shoulder of the bell and above the waist area of the bell.

QE2´s builder´s plate

Ship´s bell from RMS Aquitania and a scale model of QE2´s original steam plant propeller

Underneath *Aquitania*'s bell was a scale brass model of the original steam plant *QE2* propeller, dated 1969.

The builder's plate was an aluminium sign, measuring approximately 2.5 feet wide by 2 feet deep. The wording on the plaque read as follows:

Built and Engined by John Brown & Co (Clydebank) Ltd
now the Clydebank Division of
Upper Clyde Shipbuilders Limited Scotland

Many photographs were immediately taken of the builder's plate and RMS *Aquitania*'s ship's bell. Marius then told me that there was another ship's bell hanging from the ceiling in front of the windows which overlooked the *QE2*'s bow – on the other side of the room. I turned around to see the other bell and began making my way over to it for a closer inspection.

The QE2's builder's plate and us

As I walked over to the other bell, I stopped and my mouth dropped open wide. Stamped in black capital letters in an arc across the front of *this* bell was the name of the liner which this bell had come from– *Franconia*. I could not believe what I was looking at.

My maternal grandmother had sailed on the Cunard liner RMS *Franconia* 2 from Quebec in eastern Canada, across the North Atlantic to Liverpool in 1955. She then came home by train to Glasgow from Liverpool. Grandma had gone to Canada to visit her daughter Margaret (my mother's elder sister), who had married and then emigrated to Canada to live with Bill, a Canadian serviceman who served with the Canadian Scottish regiment and who had sailed to Britain on RMS *Mauretania* 2 in 1942, to be part of the allied invasion of Europe in 1944. When World War Two ended, Auntie Margaret had married Uncle Bill in Glasgow in 1946. Uncle Bill then went back home to British Columbia in Canada to buy a house for his new bride.

Ship's bell from RMS Franconia 2

He told me that he returned to Canada – along with thousands of other Canadian troops on RMS *Queen Elizabeth*. A year later Auntie Margaret emigrated as a war bride to Canada and sailed from Liverpool to Nova Scotia on RMS *Aquitania*, which she told me was still painted in her wartime grey paint.

As I stood staring at the *Franconia*'s ship's bell, I got the feeling that both my late maternal relatives, Grandma and Auntie Margaret, were present on either side of me and enjoying the moment too. It was such a rewarding sight to see *both* these bells.

Since RMS *Britannia* was launched in the shipyard of Robert Duncan & Company in Greenock Scotland back in 1840, there had been more than 200 Cunard liners. *Here*, in the Officers' Ward Room of the *QE2* – two decks below the bridge – were two ship's bells from Cunard liners which members of my family had sailed on in the 20th Century. This was yet another special moment for me.

There were a few other interesting artefacts displayed around the Ward Room. The original wheelhouse (portside high-pressure turbine) telegraph from RMS *Mauretania* 1907–34 which looked splendid in highly-polished brass. To the right of the *Mauretania's* telegraph, set in a large framed square was a round crankcase door, which came from one of *QE2's* engines, which had been replaced during a refit at the Blohm and Voss shipyard and engineering company in Hamburg Germany during the early 1990's.

In a glass case on the wall overlooking the QE2's bow, there were two large coin-shaped medallions which commemorated *QE2's* maiden voyage to New York in early May 1969. There were also several paintings of various Cunard liners hung on the walls around the Ward Room.

I walked slowly around the Ward Room, gazing with absolute delight at all these historical items from Cunard's liners in the past. I felt very fortunate to be allowed to see them.

RMS Mauretania´s Original Wheelhouse (Port High Pressure) Telegraph

*A crankcase door from Golf engine, replaced during a refit
at Blohm and Voss in Hamburg during the '90s.*

Maiden Voyage 2-5-1969 Commemorative plaque

It felt most peculiar, looking out of the small square front windows high up here in the Ward Room – overlooking *QE2*'s bow. I had never dreamt of looking at her bow from up here.

I thanked Marius from the bottom of my heart, for showing me all these wonderful items – especially the *QE2*'s *builder's plate*. This unexpected visit had definitely made my voyage.

Before we said goodbye to Marius, I walked over to the builder's plate and the *Aquitania's* bell to have one last look at them. I looked at the builder's plate and I said a *"Thank You"* to Saint Anthony – who once again, had let me find what I was looking for. We said goodbye to Marius, thanking him for his time and the privilege of this visit. As we left the Ward Room, we met a couple of passengers we recognised outside by the lifts. "How did you get in there?" asked the husband to us, pointing to the Ward Room.

I smiled and said, "By asking the right person – *at last!*" This couple had previously told us that they were sailing back home to Britain on the *QE2*. What a lucky couple!

There was more excitement waiting for us after our unexpected tour of the Officers' Ward Room. News greeted us that the *QM2* was sailing close to *QE2* off her starboard bow. This we had to see. We quickly made our way to the starboard Boat Deck and indeed, what a sight there was to see.

We arrived outside on the starboard Boat Deck just as the *QM2* was increasing the distance between her and the *QE2*. Luckily, I had my video camera with me, so I was able to zoom in on the *QM2* and I could clearly see many passengers on all her outside decks. The sea was so extremely smooth and calm that *QM2*'s wake was still visible in the water close to the *QE2*.

To give an indication of how close we were, without zooming in on the *QM2* – the lifeboats and davits of the *QE2* were in shot on the left-hand

RMS Queen Mary 2 with her decks full of passengers gazing at QE2

Cheerio Big Sister

side of the view-screen on my video camera, whilst I had my video-camera trained on the departing *QM2*. The big ship sailed away – just ahead of the *QE2* and widening the gap between us as she went, but always in clear sight of each other. Seeing the QM2 so close to *QE2* brought home to me the difference in size between the two liners. The *QM2* is *huge* in comparison to her older sister.

The sea was so very calm and smooth, with barely a ripple breaking the surface of the ocean. We had been very lucky to have had such a smooth and calm sea almost the entire way across the North Atlantic. We had spoken previously to a few passengers over the last few days who had complained to us about the calm sea *throughout* the voyage and who had also said that they wished the sea had "been rougher," which we both thought was a very strange remark for them to make. It would not have been very pleasant sailing through a rough sea – never mind the damage to furniture, crockery and glasses in the bars and restaurants and not forgetting the discomfort to all the passenger's stomachs!

After yet another exciting event, I decided I had better finish writing the postcards which I wanted to send home. The indoor starboard promenade deck provided a quiet and peaceful setting in which to write. When I had written all the cards which I wanted to send, I had just one blank card left. I picked up the card and wondered who to send it to?

I had written to all our close friends and family and I could not think of anyone else to send a card to. "How about *Rufus*?" suggested Ian.

Rufus was our ginger marmalade cat, whom we had rescued from an animal sanctuary several years previously. We had left Rufus in the very safe and competent hands of Derek and Jen Mansfield, who run *The Palace Cattery* – a boarding home for cats in South Stoke in Oxfordshire. Whilst we were being spoiled and treated to the high life on the *QE2*, Derek and Jen were doing the same for Rufus.

We had a photograph of Rufus which we had printed and mounted on cardboard and placed on the ledge in front of our porthole – to give us a '*reminder* of home'. "Good idea," I said. "We'll see Rufus in a couple of days when we get home anyway, but it wouldn't feel right *not* to send him one." So, Rufus received the last card.

It seemed a little odd, writing a postcard to *our* cat at *our* home address. It was a cute card and would be a nice souvenir for us to have at home. Once all the postcards had been written and left at the Purser's Office to post back to Britain, we spent the rest of the afternoon walking around the ship – until it was time to get changed into our semi-formal clothes – jacket, trousers, shirt, and tie for us men – for the last evening meal on board the *QE2*.

As it was the last night of the voyage before we arrived in New York in the morning, the dress code had been relaxed for both men and women. Once showered and dressed, we headed to the Mauretania Restaurant for dinner. Our waiting staff were there to greet us as usual and showed us to our table. "We are going to miss you all," I said to Jean – our wine waiter.

"We will miss you fellows too," said Jean, before giving me a small wine menu card with his home email address written on it. "This way, we can stay in touch," he said.

I thanked him and then opened the dinner menu, which tonight had a coloured aerial photograph of *QE2* sailing up the Hudson River on the west side of Manhattan Island on the cover. It was taken on the completion of her maiden voyage in May 1969. She was surrounded by over 25 smaller boats in the photograph, all sailing up the Hudson with her and each craft looked eager to welcome the latest in a long line of Cunarders to New York.

It was a rather sad photograph I thought, given that tomorrow morning would be *QE2*'s final arrival in this great city.

I felt greatly rewarded by the knowledge that I would be able to say for the rest of my life, that I was a passenger on the *Queen Elizabeth 2* on this; her final westbound crossing of the North Atlantic Ocean.

I opened the menu and, once again, the left-hand page was full of interesting facts under the heading: *Queen Elizabeth 2: Time to Say Goodbye.* Here are the milestones in her career with Cunard:

- 16th October 2008 would mark *QE2*'s 805th transatlantic crossing.
- *QE2*'s return journey from the Falklands Campaign in 1982 remains the longest non-stop passage of any British merchant ship.
- The shortest turnaround in New York: 5 ½ hours.
- The completion of 1,423 voyages.
- The travelling of 5,808,026 million nautical miles – more than any other ship ever.
- The carrying of almost 2 ½ million passengers.
- The completion of 806 Atlantic crossings.
- 710 calls at New York.
- 726 calls at Southampton.
- The completion of 25 full world cruises.
- The completion of ten "extended" voyages.
- Under the command of 25 captains.

Having quickly read all this interesting information, my eyes turned to the right-hand page of the menu card to choose from the – appropriately named – selections of the *American Dinner*.

For starters I chose the Philadelphia pepper pot, which is a thick stew of beef tripe with vegetables, pepper, and other seasonings. For my main course I chose a grilled rib steak of Kansas beef with Cajun spiced café de Paris butter with oven-roasted and glazed root vegetables, broiled tomato and country fried potatoes.

My waitress asked me "If I would like custard?" – as she served my Boston cream cake sponge with rum sauce which I had ordered for dessert.

"Yes please," I answered. She produced a long thin silver spoon and deftly cut out the centre of the sponge and she then poured warm custard into the deep circular hole which she had just made in the sponge cake.

"Wow!" I said, impressed. "You have done that before." She smiled at my delight. "I have had some practice," she said.

Our last dinner on *QE2* was as enjoyable and memorable as all the previous meals. It remained true to say that the food on *QE2* was *wonderful*!

We left the Mauretania Restaurant and walked to The Golden Lion for a drink. Ray Terry and his jazz band had not started playing yet. After finishing our drinks, we headed back to our stateroom: intending to put our menus for that evening's dinner into a drawer in the dressing table which held the menus for the previous five evening meals which we had eaten on the *QE2*. But we had a surprise waiting for us when we walked into our room.

Lying on each bed was a thin cardboard box, approximately one inch deep by twelve and a quarter-inches wide. There was a coloured print on the lid showing several of Cunard's famous liners from the past with *QE2* leading the fleet. The heading on the lid read in large capital letters:

QE2: **TAKING HER PLACE IN HISTORY.**

Beside this box were two large certificates, both embossed with gold edging which read;

**"Cunard celebrated (*our*) presence on board
Queen Elizabeth 2 on her final westbound crossing
in tandem with *Queen Mary 2*.
10 – 16 October 2008
Southampton to New York."**

The two certificates each had our full names printed at the top of the certificate and underneath our name, the Cunard logo was printed in gold with Cunard printed in red below that.

We took all our menus from the dressing table drawer and carefully slid them all into the box. The menus all fitted perfectly along with the two certificates. "I've seen that print on the box-lid before," I said to Ian. "Although, I've never seen it with the *QE2* at the front of all the other liners."

The *Queen's Mary & Elizabeth* were drawn sailing just behind the *QE2* with *Caronia, Mauretania 2, Franconia 3* and half a dozen other famous Cunard liners bringing up the rear. There was a small *QE2 "Farewell Celebration"* logo in the top right-hand corner of the print on the lid.

We had received a small round white China dish with this logo on it which was waiting for us when we arrived back in our stateroom a few nights previously. Nowadays, it hangs proudly on the wall in our kitchen at home.

"The box will keep all the menus and certificates safe from being damaged," Ian said to me. I agreed and looked rather apprehensively at all the white paper shopping bags embossed with Cunard's name in red on the front of them, which contained all the souvenirs we had bought, as well as presents which all lay on the floor at the bottom of my bed.

"I'm so very glad we borrowed Christine's big case to get all this stuff home," I said again to Ian. "Definitely!" he agreed.

Once we had placed the menus and certificates safely into the *"Farewell Celebration"* box, we went back to The Golden Lion for a few more drinks, before deciding we ought to finish packing the last few items and as we were planning on getting up early the next day to witness our arrival in New York: it was time for an early night.

As our day was due to commence very early, I set the alarm on my mobile phone to go off at 04:30AM and climbed into my bed. My mind was racing: thinking of our arrival in New York the following morning and after tossing and turning a few times, I finally drifted off to sleep.

CHAPTER 7

Voyage end

Thursday, 16th October 2008

Weather: Cloudy on arrival in New York with a
few sunny spells throughout the day.

I awoke just before my alarm and went to get a drink of water. I walked back into our bedroom and looked out of the porthole. What a surprise I had!

We had obviously reached land as I saw the headlights of a car driving along a coastal road. I found out later, that this road was part of the State of New Jersey, which lies on the southern border of New York State on the east coast of America. I have never been so surprised to see a car with its headlights on! After sailing – *almost alone* – across the North Atlantic for almost five and a half days, with only *QM2* and a cargo ship to witness our voyage, it was very unexpected to see a car *and* land.

I woke up Ian and put the kettle on to make a coffee, which we quickly gulped down, before heading up on deck. We were just in time to witness *QE2* sailing under the Verrazzano-Narrows Bridge, which links the New York City boroughs of Brooklyn and Staten Island. This bridge is also well-known for being the longest suspension bridge in the Western Hemisphere and it has a very elegant span. From where we were standing on the portside Boat Deck, it looked as if the top of *QE2*'s mast would clip the underside of the bridge.

It did not of course, and she sailed smoothly under the bridge and began her journey across a stretch of water known as *The Upper Bay*, passing the Statue of Liberty on a small island which lay off *QE2*'s portside. This small island is called *Liberty Island* and holds the world-famous statue on a stone pedestal.

Lady Liberty was holding her lighted torch in her raised right hand, with a tablet bearing the date of the Declaration of Independence in 1776 in her left hand and is an instantly recognisable figure to countless millions upon millions of immigrants and travellers to the United States of America.

I had always associated the Statue of Liberty with New York. But in fact, Liberty Island is on the New Jersey side of *The Upper Bay* – just a few miles from Jersey City itself. The statue was lit from the ground and she really stood out and was a most welcome sight. Her torch was lit too, giving the impression of a flame.

We were very close to completing our voyage. We had reached America, after what must have been one of the smoothest crossings the *QE2* had ever had – in all her 39 years of sailing the North Atlantic Ocean.

The *QE2* sailed smoothly towards Manhattan Island and as it was still dark, the lights which were on in a lot of the many skyscrapers which dominate the Manhattan skyline, lent credence to New York's reputation – as *the city which never sleeps*. Bearing in mind that it was just approaching 6:00AM, to see so many lights on in the elegant skyscrapers which lined the west side of Manhattan Island was quite wonderful to see.

Instantly recognisable was the shiny vertex of the Chrysler Building which, although it lies on Manhattan's east side, is so tall that it towered above many of the skyscrapers around it and could easily be seen from the Hudson River on the west side of Manhattan. It was briefly the world's tallest building when it opened in 1930 but it lost that title to the Empire State Building, when it opened 11 months later.

To be sailing up the Hudson River, passing Manhattan's elegant skyline on board the last Cunard liner which had been built in Britain was such a memorable occasion for me.

As a life-long fan of Cunard's great liners from the past, it really does not come much better than this!

Finally, the *QE2* began to slowly turn into an empty pier: we had arrived at Pier 90 in Manhattan. Pier 90 – at over 1,000 feet in length – had been specifically built in the early 1930s – opening in 1935 to accommodate the new liners then being planned around the world. This was the pier where RMS *Queen Mary* had docked at the end of her maiden voyage in 1936. This was yet another proud moment for me.

Daylight quickly arrived and we took numerous photographs of the New York landscape as viewed from the *QE2* as well as of the surrounding piers – We

View of USS Intrepid in Pier 86

asked a lady who had joined us outside the Funnel Bar, to take a photograph of ourselves – in front of the Funnel Bar with *QE2*'s iconic funnel above us.

To our right, docked nearby in Pier 86, was the aircraft carrier *USS Intrepid*. This aircraft carrier was built in 1943 and saw extensive service during World War Two; including surviving no less than five kamikaze attacks and one torpedo strike. She was decommissioned shortly after the end of the war and now lies quietly in Pier 86 as the *Intrepid Sea, Air & Space Museum*, on the west side of Manhattan Island. There are several military aircraft displayed on board the *Intrepid*, plus a cruise missile submarine beside it. Also displayed onboard the *Intrepid* is a USAF SR-71 Blackbird long-range high-altitude reconnaissance aircraft which is the fastest aircraft ever built. It certainly looked very sleek.

The sun was starting to break through the morning mist and the clouds in the sky around us were beginning to break up too. It was a pleasantly mild day in New York and the city seemed to be well and truly alive now. You could hear the distant hum of traffic from the roads in the city.

Daylight view of Manhattan from QE2's starboard aft Sun Deck

Hello New York!

Two happy passengers

We had to wait until our colour – blue – disembarkation ticket was announced over the ship's tannoy, so we did a little exploring again and found ourselves in front of several tall glass display cases which we had not seen before – not far from The Golden Lion pub.

These display cases were attached to the walls and their contents were a dream to witness for any Cunard Line enthusiast. Almost every souvenir which Cunard had ever made was displayed in these cases.

Everything from playing cards to spoons, teacups and saucers to China ashtrays. There were silver trays, jigsaws of either of Cunard's first two *Queens: Mary* and *Elizabeth* and quite a few models of other Cunard liners too. All were on display inside the glass cases. I saw a tin and recognised the print on the lid of *RMS Queen Mary*. The tin was a slightly different shape to the one which I have at home but the print of "*Mary*" was the same.

Eventually, the call went out over the ship's tannoy system for passengers with blue disembarkation tickets to make their way to the Midship Lobby to disembark *QE2*. I stopped when we got to the lobby and took a lingering, long last look all around me. "I am really going to miss you *QE2*," I said to her, before walking over to the exit door.

I paused at the exit doorway and thanked her for getting Ian and me and all our fellow passengers and crew, safely to New York. As I stepped out of the *QE2* and onto the gangway, I turned to face her and patted her hull plates farewell. Then I leaned over to her and gently kissed the hull plating at the side of the Lobby doorway goodbye. I must admit to having a lump in my throat as I did this.

I followed Ian down the gangway, but paused when I got to the bottom – it had suddenly hit me that my next step would copy what countless millions of immigrants, travellers and visitors to America had done over hundreds of years – set foot in America. Standing outside on land and looking back at Pier 90, I gazed up at the *QE2* and admired her size – she looked huge now, when standing beside her.

QE2 docked in Pier 90 Manhattan, at the end of her final
westbound crossing; Thursday 16th October 2008

I noticed she was flying her red paying-off pennant from her mast. A paying-off pennant is flown from a ship's mast to mark the end of a ship's commission. The pennant's length is calculated at one foot for every year of the ship's service and thus *QE2*'s pennant was 39 feet in length.

"I'm really going to miss her," I said to Ian. "Me too," he replied, "at least we'll always have the memories of crossing the North Atlantic Ocean on her." I nodded in agreement and we made our way into the terminal, where we joined a long queue of our fellow passengers to get our passports checked and stamped.

We then had to make our way outside, to where a coach was waiting on Twelfth Avenue ready to take about 20 of *QE2*'s passengers on a tour of Manhattan's famous sights. Before we stepped onto the coach, I turned to take one last look at the *QE2*, lying peacefully docked at the left-hand side of Pier 90.

Ian quickly took several final photographs of her, before boarding the coach. The *QE2* had been our home for the last five and a half days and it was sad to be saying goodbye to her – it felt as though she had become a very good friend.

As I took one last look at her – the most loved and most famous ocean liner in the world – I was reminded of Cunard's famous advertising slogan from the 1950's, which I said to myself *then* and I will paraphrase that slogan here – with the addition of an emphasis, as it seems to me to accurately sum up the experience of crossing the North Atlantic Ocean on the *QE2* – the last British-built Cunard Ocean liner:

*"Getting there was **more** than half the fun."*

THE END

Acknowledgements

On a personal level I would like to thank:

Ian Wilson
Ian McNaught CVO MNM FNI
Marius Cerniauskas
Jim Checkosky
Henry Cheung
Jenni Cook
Cunard Line
Eric Douglass
Michael Gannon
Jenny and Derek Mansfield
Christine Massey
Nicholas Taylor
Wikipedia

www.ingramcontent.com/pod-product-compliance
Lightning Source LLC
Chambersburg PA
CBHW050036040726
47599CB00015B/1697